Designed by Flowerpot Press in Franklin, TN.
www.FlowerpotPress.com
Designer: Jonas Fearon Bell
Editor: Johannah Gilman Paiva
PAB-0808-0141
ISBN: 978-1-4867-0834-5
Made in China/Fabriqué en Chine

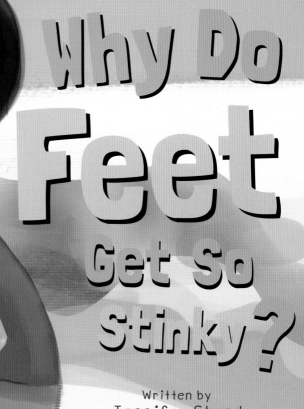

Why Do Feet Get So Stinky?

Written by
Jennifer Shand

Illustrated by
Daniele Fabbri

The human body is awesome!

It allows us to do so many things and think so many thoughts.
As you learn more about the human body, you will make endless
discoveries that will intrigue and amaze you!

Why do CHILDREN lose their BABY TEETH?

Is it because they eat too much CANDY
and don't BRUSH their teeth?

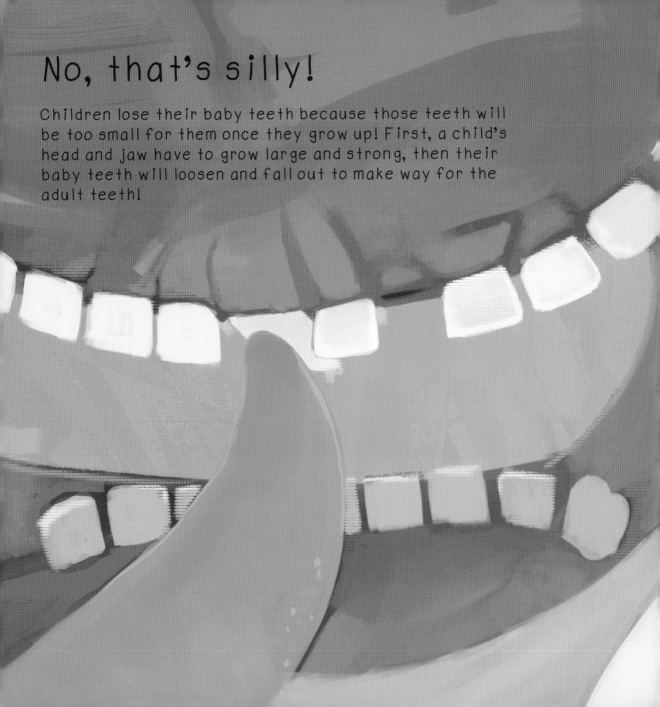

No, that's silly!

Children lose their baby teeth because those teeth will be too small for them once they grow up! First, a child's head and jaw have to grow large and strong, then their baby teeth will loosen and fall out to make way for the adult teeth!

Why do FEET get so STINKY?

Is it because SKUNKS sneak into our rooms at night
and SPRAY our feet?

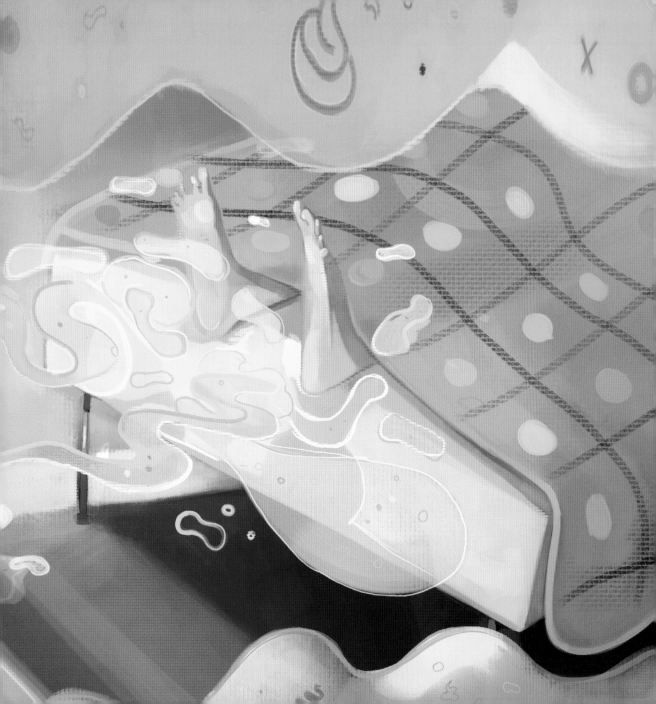

No, that's silly!

Feet get stinky because they have more sweat glands than any other part of the body. Sweat glands are important because they keep our body temperature from getting too hot.

Sweat can become very smelly.
Being inside socks and shoes adds
to the stinky problem because they
lock in the stink and keep out the
fresh air.

Why do BELLIES have BELLY BUTTONS?

Is it to be able to STORE THINGS in them?

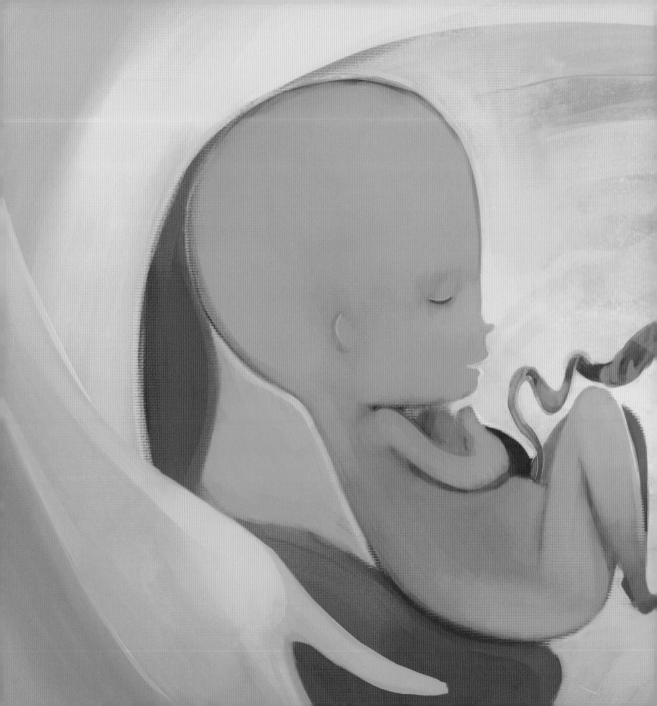

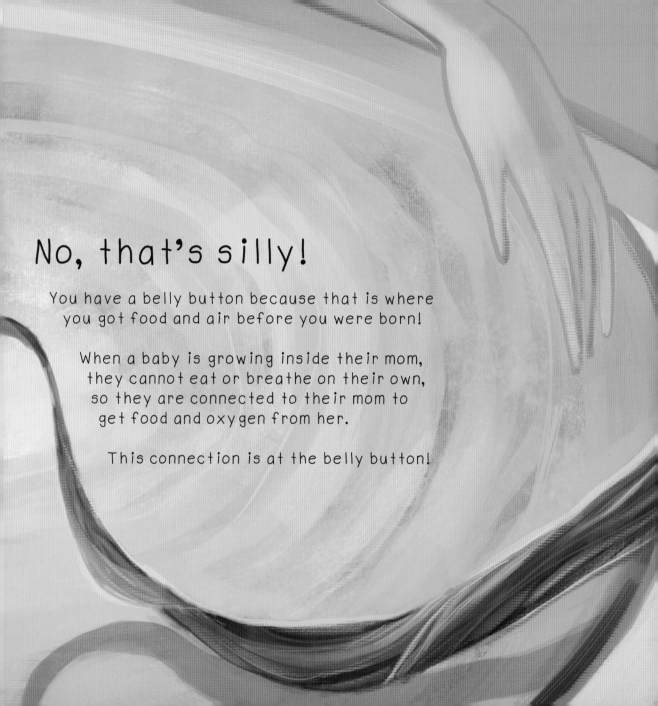

No, that's silly!

You have a belly button because that is where
you got food and air before you were born!

When a baby is growing inside their mom,
they cannot eat or breathe on their own,
so they are connected to their mom to
get food and oxygen from her.

This connection is at the belly button!

Why do TUMMIES rumble and make GROWLING noises?

Is it because there is a TINY BEAR
inside your belly that loves to GROWL?

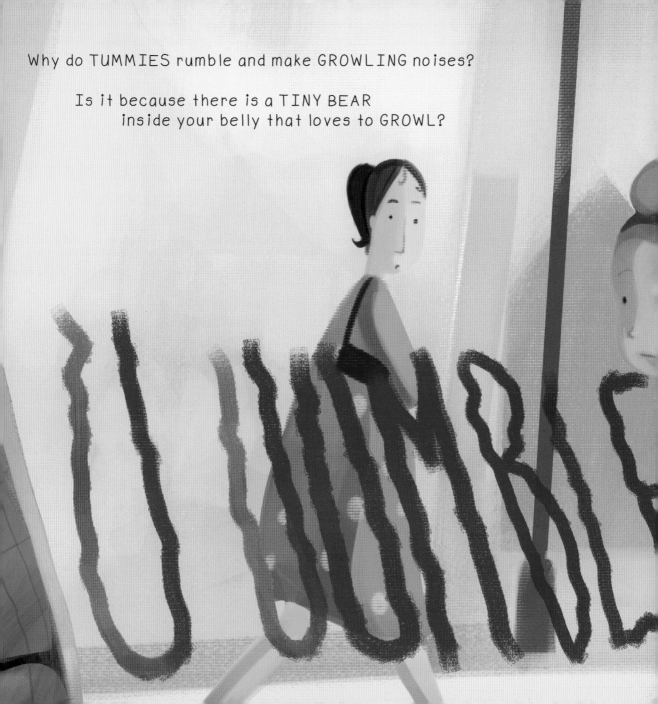

No, that's silly!

Tummies rumble because they are doing a lot of work!

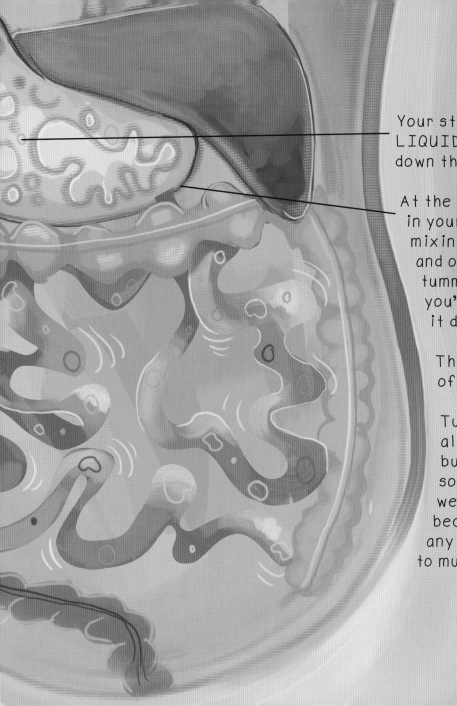

Your stomach releases LIQUIDS that help break down the food you eat.

At the same time, MUSCLES in your stomach squeeze, mixing the liquids, air, and other gases in your tummy with the food you've eaten, to break it down even further.

This makes a lot of noise!

Tummies rumble all through the day, but the rumbling sounds louder when we are hungry, because there isn't any food in our belly to muffle the growling.

Why do some PEOPLE have FRECKLES?

Is it because they COLORED on themselves with a PERMANENT marker?

No, that's silly!

People have freckles because other people in their family have freckles, too!

We inherit all of our traits from our parents, and freckles are just one of those traits!

We get more freckles on our bodies when we have been out in the sun, because the sun activates melanin, a protein in our bodies that affects the color of our skin.

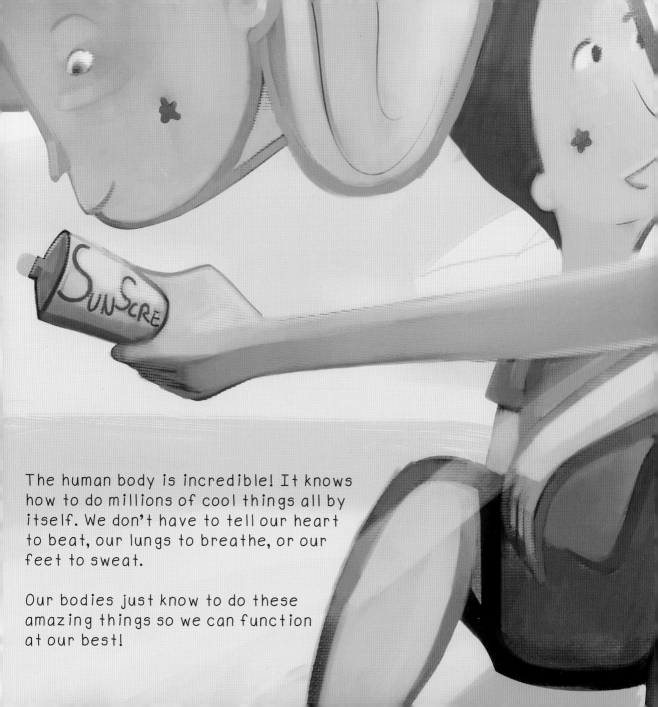

The human body is incredible! It knows how to do millions of cool things all by itself. We don't have to tell our heart to beat, our lungs to breathe, or our feet to sweat.

Our bodies just know to do these amazing things so we can function at our best!